Original title:
Existentialism with a Side of Fries

Copyright © 2025 Creative Arts Management OÜ
All rights reserved.

Author: Adrian Caldwell
ISBN HARDBACK: 978-1-80566-017-0
ISBN PAPERBACK: 978-1-80566-312-6

Crooked Paths and Curly Fries

In a world where questions swirl,
I munch on fries that twist and twirl.
The meaning of life, I seek to find,
But ketchup's the answer, or so I'm inclined.

Burgers and laughter, a whimsical feast,
Is happiness fleeting, or just a tease?
With each crispy bite, my worries depart,
Who needs enlightenment when there's a tart?

The cosmos cackles with each fry I dip,
A side of joy on this cosmic trip.
Why ponder the void when I can indulge?
In grease and giggles, my thoughts can bulge.

So I'll dance through life, with saucy delight,
Embracing absurdity, with all of my might.
In this carnival quest, with laughter and sighs,
I'll savor each moment, like curly fries.

Biting Into the Unknowable

In a world that's all fried,
Questions bubble like grease.
What's the point of this ride?
(And please pass the cheese.)

Lost in thoughts, I munch on,
Is life a meal or a snack?
Am I the king or a pawn?
These fries won't ever come back.

Crispy Layers of Thought

Peeling back each crisp skin,
Like layers of my own mind.
What's beneath this golden grin?
More fries? What will I find?

Each bite brings a new fear,
What if the ketchup is wrong?
I dip and devour with cheer,
But life sings a confusing song.

The Sauciness of Existence

Existence is quite messy,
Like sauce dripped on a plate.
Do I leave it or get dressy?
Who knew fries could question fate?

Every bite holds a secret,
Drowned in ranch, sweet and thick.
Life's riddles I must tweak it,
Yet I just want a quick fix.

Days and Dippers

Some days I'm extra crispy,
Other days just a fry.
Life dips me in something fishy,
Is my purpose to comply?

With each day's sweet or sour,
The fry basket overflows.
Searching for hidden power,
While munching on all my woes.

Salted Doubts

Amidst the crunch, we munch away,
Wondering why we think this way.
A side of fries, a side of thought,
Is meaning found, or just bought?

Seasoned thoughts in ketchup pools,
As we navigate our fast food rules.
The taste of life, a savory jest,
What's better, living or a quest?

Renegotiating Reality

Reality's a burger stacked,
But often leaves our minds quite hacked.
New deals on fries, fresh and hot,
What's real or fake? I haven't a jot.

A bun of being, soft and warm,
In this café, I find my charm.
With every bite, perceptions sway,
Do I even need to stay today?

Fryers of Fate

In a fryer's oil, my choices swim,
The world outside feels so grim.
Each golden chip, a fateful slice,
Dip it in sauce, or consider your price.

Paths are crispy, some are soggy,
Life's a snack that's often foggy.
Will I toast to my own despair,
Or savor each bite, without a care?

The Dilemma of Dips

A tray of options, sauces galore,
Pick a dip, or just ask for more!
Ranch or honey, sassy or plain,
Each choice I make drives me insane.

Dip it low or take it high,
Will this snack help me get by?
In condiments, reflection lies,
The meaning thickens, like fry surprise.

The Crunch of Choices

In a world of golden fries,
I ponder life with cheesy sighs.
Do I dip or do I drench?
These thoughts, a tasty wrench.

Between the salt and sweet delight,
My heart's a burger, oh what a sight!
Each crunch a question, crisp and bold,
With every bite, new truths unfold.

Nuggets of Insight Beyond the Tray.

Chicken nuggets in a messy heap,
Stirring thoughts that chase my sleep.
Are we just bites in life's big feast?
Or savory dreams that bloat the beast?

Dipped in sauces of urgent fear,
Each nugget whispers, loud and clear.
What's the dip for this grand quest?
A side of wisdom? That's the best!

Fries in the Face of Infinity

When the universe seems vast and wide,
I munch on fries with crunchy pride.
Each slender stick a question asked,
In this crispy world, I'm happily masked.

Why ponder deep when you can snack?
The answers hide in salt and crack.
For every fry, a thought unspools,
A life of laughter, bending rules.

The Sizzle of Being

Hear the sizzle, life ablaze,
In the pan where dreams are grazed.
What's the meaning, oh so spry?
Just spice it up—let flavors fly!

In every fry, a moment's glow,
A dance of souls in ebb and flow.
With ketchup smiles and onion rings,
I find the joy that living brings.

The Burger of Being

In a bun of thoughts, we play,
Lettuce dreams and cheese decay.
Patty patter, life's a fry,
Bite the question, dare to try.

Sipping shakes of fleeting time,
Ketchup laughs, a little rhyme.
Onions layer truth and jest,
Is this burger life's grand quest?

Underneath the Salted Skin

Beneath the crunch, a world awaits,
With every bite, the heart debates.
Are we the fries, or just the salt?
Dipping thoughts in rivers of malt.

Laughing at the grease we bear,
Fried reflections in the air.
What's the meaning, crispy and bright?
Munching on chaos, day turns to night.

Of Sauces and Searchings

In the pool of ranch, I dream a lot,
Sriracha whispers, "You're not what you're not."
Honey mustard thinks it's wise,
Mixing up truths in a savory guise.

Dip your worries, swirl your fears,
BBQ jokes drown in our tears.
Life's a feast, so take your share,
With every sauce, a truth laid bare.

A Plate Full of Paradoxes

A burger's weight in fleeting thought,
Greasy truths we never sought.
Fries of fate on dishes wide,
Drown in condiments, no need to hide.

What's the verdict? Crunch or chew?
Philosophy served with a view.
Burger flipping, life's a game,
For each joy, a side of blame.

French Fries in the Void

In a realm where thoughts collide,
Fries float by without a guide.
Ketchup dreams on nothing's plate,
We munch on fate, and laugh at fate.

Lost in thoughts like fries in oil,
Grease of life, we dare to toil.
Dipping minds in spicy quests,
We crunch our fears through tasty tests.

Chasing shadows of the fry,
Philosophers in ketchup shy.
With every bite, we ponder why,
As crispy echoes dance and fly.

Among the stars, a fryer spins,
Universe of salty wins.
In the void, we munch away,
Fried absurdity on display.

Frying Pan Philosophies

In a skillet of thought, we fry,
Sizzling questions, oh my, oh my!
With spatulas for ideas bold,
We flip our worries, truths unfold.

Why do fries so often crave,
A dip in wisdom, quite the rave?
Oil of thought, we stir and fry,
Lipstick stains on questions spry.

While cooking life in heat so high,
We season doubts and wing them sly.
With laughter, we toss what we know,
A feast of thoughts, all in a show.

In this pan of life, we dine,
Smirking at what we call divine.
With every crunch, we savor fear,
Fry on, my friend, and drink a beer.

Taste Buds of the Mind

What's the flavor of existence?
A sprinkle here, a dash of distance.
Brains like fries, so crispy fried,
Dipped in questions, do we bide?

In the kitchen of the mind,
All the spices we can find.
Sautéed dreams and salted tears,
Feeding laughter, calming fears.

Every bite's a thought to feast,
Chewing on what matters least.
Life's absurd, yet we delight,
With every fry comes new insight.

So grab a plate, let's fill it high,
With musings, jokes, and grace—oh my!
Taste the crunch, give it a whirl,
Savor life in a fried swirl.

The Crunch of Consciousness

Crispy thoughts, they crack and pop,
In the mind's fryer, they'll never stop.
Fries of wisdom, hot and bold,
Hungry hearts will never fold.

In the crunch of life's sweet snack,
We ponder paths, there's no way back.
Every fry holds secret lore,
In the grease, our dreams explore.

With ketchup minds we take the leap,
Diving deep, the flavors steep.
Nougat thoughts, and chocolate dreams,
Whipped up in absurdity's schemes.

Laughing loud while crunching down,
In the fryer, we wear the crown.
A banquet full of silly cheer,
Life's crispy truths are always near.

Chasing Shadows and Snack Baskets

In a world of greasy dreams,
I chase shapes of laughter,
Philosophy in ketchup streams,
While pondering my after.

Fries on trays do dance and sway,
With joy, they hold my fate,
I wander through this fried buffet,
Oven-baked or microwave? Fate!

The shadows of my choices loom,
Like empty boxes in the night,
With every bite, I'll find my room,
Snack baskets filled with sheer delight.

A paradox of salty bliss,
My mind, a hungry pot,
Who knew a fry could bring such bliss,
In questions that I've got?

Meaning Beyond the Meal

In lunches past, I've searched for depth,
But crisp potatoes steal the show,
Conversations at my table heft,
Over dips and heights of nacho flow.

With every crunch, a thought appears,
Why are we here? What's the score?
But all my friends just laugh with cheers,
As they devour fries and more.

I ponder fate in every bite,
While munching on my golden stash,
Each fry a fate, each dip a right,
And all my worries turn to ash.

So grab a plate, don't miss the fun,
Let's fry the thoughts that make us fall,
For at our table, we are one,
Chasing meaning through it all.

The Crunch that Shook the Soul

One bite into the spud's embrace,
I ponder life with all its cheer,
The crunch resounds, a sweet bass case,
As fries declare, "Have no fear."

In crispy layers, truths unwind,
The universe in frying oil,
From trusting grease, we're all aligned,
Salted wisdom in the toil.

The fryer hums a playful tune,
While ketchup smiles from its jar,
We laugh at fate beneath the moon,
Life's a banquet, here we spar.

So take a bite and join the fun,
Philosophy, a feast divine,
Each fry consumed, we've just begun,
To savor life, like sweet design.

Frying the Big Questions

What is the meaning of this fry?
Is it fate or just a chance?
As I ponder and devour, oh my,
My soul begins to dance.

The oil bubbles with each thought,
What am I worth in grease and salt?
I fry my doubts, they sizzle hot,
As laughter becomes my vault.

With waves of flavor washing over,
I munch on dreams, fried crisp, not stale,
In each golden lump, a chance for closure,
Life's riddles served with ketchup trail.

So let's not fret while eating fries,
Joy's hidden in a crunchy guise,
In every bite, a sweet surprise,
Frying big questions, chasing skies!

A Side of Questions

Why do we fry and why do we bake?
Life's just a buffet, for goodness' sake.
Chasing the flavor, we lose our way,
Searching for meaning in a cold tray.

Are these crispy curls all that we crave?
Can fries dig deeper, or just misbehave?
The ketchup's a puzzle, a slippery clue,
As we dip and we ponder, what's really true?

In a world of fast snacks and lonesome bites,
Do we savor life or just chase the lights?
Burgers speak truths from their sesame crowns,
Yet here in the wrappers, we find our frowns.

As I munch on my doubts, they turn into crumbs,
Resisting the urge to see where it comes.
With each golden fry, these questions ensue,
Is it fries that are deep or am I too?

Unraveled Thoughts and Golden Sticks

Fries on my plate, and thoughts in my head,
Like tangled up strings, they won't be misled.
Each crispy stick whispers, 'Life isn't dull,'
But the more that I ponder, I just feel a pull.

The fryer's a trap where dreams go to fry,
Seasoned with laughter, I sit and I sigh.
Why does the universe swirl in a pan?
Do potatoes consider the fate of the plan?

With oil bubbling questions, I ponder and chew,
A golden delight with a side serving true.
Am I the side dish, or am I the feast?
In this esoteric meal, I'm confused at least.

As I spill out my thoughts with each crispy bite,
Are these fries the truth or just a delight?
In a world of the absurd, my wisdom fries,
With a sprinkle of laughter, beneath clear blue skies.

A Solitary Fritter

In my lonesome munch, a fritter stands proud,
Whispering secrets that echo aloud.
Is my snack the answer or just the tease?
Each crunch is a question that begs to appease.

With a sauce on the side, I dip in my fears,
Laughing at moments that danced through the years.
Is this batter of mine stuffed with purpose or air?
The crunch is profound, but where's my flair?

As the world spins around in a deep fryer's fate,
I ponder my choices, debating my plate.
A solitary fritter in a platter of plight,
Could this be my calling — my snack or the light?

I laugh at the irony, munching away,
This crispy little gem keeps the darkness at bay.
So here's to the fritter, amusing and bright,
With each tasty bite, I'm savoring the night.

Beyond the Plate

What lies beyond just salt and a shake?
Is life just a patty on a warm bread baked?
We nibble on dreams like a burger so wide,
Yet more than mere calories, be our guide.

Beyond the plate is a universe steeped,
In grease and in laughter, where secrets are kept.
Are fries our companions or simply a thrill?
Their crunch echoes truths that can't be fulfilled.

In the realm of the culinary, spirits do dance,
As I take my last bite, will I leave it to chance?
With a side of reflection, my hunger remains,
In the kitchen of life, I'm stirring my gains.

So let's raise a toast to the meal we create,
With sauces unseen, and flavors ornate.
In every fried morsel, a giggle or two,
For beyond the plate lies the mystery — you.

Philosophical Crinkles

In the fryer of thought, we ponder our fate,
Fries whisper truths while we sit on a plate.
Crispy questions rise with a side of delight,
Dancing on tongues, they sparkle so bright.

Dipping in ketchup, we laugh at the mess,
What's life without condiments, more or less?
Potatoes and pondering, a savory blend,
In this world of flavor, we pretend we're transcend.

So we crunch through existence, one fry at a time,
Seeking the answers, but no reason, no rhyme.
Each bite like a moment, so fleeting and sly,
In the deep fryer of life, we all just pass by.

The Taste of Ephemeral Moments

Life's a fast food drive-thru, what do you choose?
A bite of this chaos, in flavors we lose.
Crisp like the laughter that dances through air,
What's gone in a heartbeat, it's hard not to care.

Fries by the dozen, we pick and we share,
Moments like morsels, they vanish, unfair.
With a side of absurdity, we savor the joke,
As we munch through the mystery, laughter we're woke.

In the fleeting, we find that we're never alone,
Flavors entwined, like the thoughts we have grown.
So let's dip into life with a sprinkle of glee,
For each crunchy question contains a small spree.

What Lies Beneath the Golden Crust

Beneath all the glimmer, what secrets remain?
A spud's inner turmoil, an existential strain.
Gold on the surface, but what's deep inside?
A crunchy facade hides the fears we can't bide.

Fries can be fickle, though tasty and warm,
Like thoughts that abound in a whimsical storm.
Do we dare to uncover, each layer we peel?
In oil and in laughter, maybe truth's just a meal.

With every sound crunch, does the wisdom emerge?
Or is it just grease that fuels our own urge?
As we dine on the dreams, let's embrace every bite,
For the flavor of pondering is often a sight.

Musings on the Edge of a Plate

On the edge of the plate, where thoughts come to play,
Fries teeter and tumble, as if they might sway.
A sprinkle of salt, a dash of the weird,
Existence is fried, but it's mostly endeared.

Do the fries have feelings? Or just cravings for fun?
Philosophers munching, we bite one by one.
With laughter and grease, our theories unfold,
In a world made of snacks, we're whimsical, bold.

So let's raise our forks high, toast to the absurd,
With each crispy morsel, let's savor the word.
For on this grand platter, with joy we partake,
In the realm of the silly, let's dance till we ache.

The Meaning Beneath the Grease

In a world where spuds get fried,
We ponder while our waistbands slide.
What's life's meaning, you may ask,
Is it in burgers or a crispy mask?

Each fry a question, golden and bold,
Do we find answers or just more gold?
Dipped in ketchup, thoughts come alive,
While grease-stained worries dive and jive.

The fryer sings, a symphony so sweet,
As I munch on fate wrapped in a treat.
Beneath the surface, with each bite,
Lies a giggle tucked in the midnight light.

We ask if purpose sizzles or fries,
Or simply dances among buttered sighs.
As I crunch on dreams, savored and bright,
I wonder if existence is just a late-night bite.

A Side of Life's Questions

Life's a menu, choices galore,
Do I want the fries, or something more?
With every order, a question arrives,
Is it the food, or how one thrives?

Balancing health with a piece of cake,
A side of thoughts, do I dare partake?
With each crispy crunch, I ponder away,
Is it now or later, this game we play?

Beneath the surface of oily delight,
Are we seeking answers in every bite?
Or is it just humor that fills the plate?
One can only laugh, as we contemplate fate.

I dig into fries and ask with a grin,
What's the flavor of life that's buried within?
With salt on my tongue, I bet it's sublime,
It's funny how joy can taste just like thyme.

The Absurdity of French Fries

In a land where taters take a fry,
I ask the universe, oh my, oh my!
Each crispy morsel, a laugh I find,
A side of chaos, with thoughts intertwined.

Are we just slices in a greasy pot,
Wondering if we mean something or not?
As I dip my fries in that creamy pool,
I ponder if life's a cosmic duel.

The absurdity bubbles, it's quite a show,
As I munch on musings, I start to glow.
In a takeout box, my cares take flight,
Life's a jest, and I'm feeling light!

With every bite, I chuckle with glee,
Is it fate or just chance? Oh, can't you see?
In the wacky world of spuds and glee,
There lies my truth served hot and free.

Thoughts Served Hot and Salty

In a diner of dreams, I take a seat,
Where thoughts are served up crispy and sweet.
I ponder the universe, thick with grease,
While munching on wisdom, I seek release.

Fries piled high, a tower of fate,
Each crunch a question, I contemplate.
With salt on my tongue and laughs in the air,
Is life a joke, or a circus affair?

Philosophy drizzled with ranch so fine,
As I dip my doubts, am I crossing a line?
Beneath every fry is a story untold,
In this odd banquet, my heart feels bold.

So let's feast on thoughts, let's not take a bite,
Of seriousness, just a sprinkle of light.
With laughter as fuel and fries at my side,
I'll navigate life's ride, arms open wide.

Contemplations at the Fast Food Window

Beneath the golden arches, I wait,
Life's questions sizzle on my plate.
Do I choose the fries or the big shake?
In this moment, I ponder my fate.

Burgers whisper secrets, dressed in glaze,
While I wrestle with the end of days.
Is it freedom found in a crispy bite?
Or just a hunger biting at my might?

The drive-thru speaker crackles like fate,
As I navigate choices on my plate.
A milkshake of thoughts, thick and absurd,
Where meaning and sodium are freshly stirred.

In the end, with a smile large and wide,
I triumphantly take my joy in stride.
For here, in the chaos of sauce and bun,
I dance with my thoughts; all's said and done.

Life in the Drive-Thru Lane

In the queue of cars, a life unfolds,
With dreams as soft as warm burger folds.
Questions arise while I sip my Coke,
Is my destiny written in the yolk?

The menu's a riddle, all wrapped in cheese,
Like my mind, it sways in the summer breeze.
Fries in the basket, a side of delight,
Yet loneliness sneaks in with each bite.

Tick-tock the clock, the spirit of haste,
What's worth more? The fries or the taste?
Am I just a number, a face in the crowd?
Or a philosopher driving, so blissfully loud?

At last I'm served, with a wink from the cook,
In between orders, we write our own book.
Through grease and confusion, we'll find some fun,
In this drive-thru lane, we're never done.

Between Ketchup and Conundrums

A bottle of ketchup, sleek and red,
Stands tall like a thought inside my head.
Is it tangy satisfaction I seek?
Or a deeper taste that feels less bleak?

As fries tumble down like bits of fate,
I dip them in meaning, oh, isn't it great?
But what is that flavor? I can't quite say,
Perhaps it's just life in a witty display.

In this diner of thought, we laugh and we cry,
With questions served hot, and answers awry.
Can the punchline come from a side of slaw?
Or a milkshake filled with a moment of awe?

So dip deep and ponder, in sauces divine,
For meaning's at the bottom of each french fry line.
Between bursts of laughter and bites of bliss,
Life's cheeky mysteries persist with a kiss.

The Void and the Vending Machine

Staring at snacks through the glass so clear,
A void of choices brings me cheer.
Is it chips or candy that feeds my soul?
Or are they both just a hole in the whole?

The little lights shimmer like stars at night,
Suggesting the universe's sheer delight.
I ponder my existence as I press A2,
Is the answer contained in the snacks I pursue?

A crunchy dilemma wrapped in foil's hue,
With every quarter, I muse what's true.
An abyss of flavors now dances in sight,
Yet questions remain — delight or a fright?

So I'll drop my coins and celebrate fate,
As I munch on my choices, delicious and great.
In this curious cycle of munching divine,
I find life's meaning in snacks and in time.

Transience and Tater Tots

Tater tots sizzle, life's little tease,
Crispy edges dancing in the breeze.
We munch on fleeting joys, oh so grand,
As ketchup pools, Time slips from hand.

In a world of fries, what's truly right?
The universe spins, day turns to night.
These bite-sized wonders, they nod and sway,
While we ponder why we're here today.

Palate of Perception

Life's a buffet, with choices galore,
Fries on the side, but what's at the core?
Bubble and fry, we laugh at our fate,
With every dip, we're questioning fate.

A burger of thoughts, it's stacked high,
We chew on absurdities, oh me, oh my!
But amidst this feast, we still taste the void,
In mustard and chaos, we're mostly destroyed.

Frying the Fabric of Existence

The fryer hums, with secrets it keeps,
As we ponder what lies beneath our sleeps.
Potatoes in oil, what's real, what's fake?
Shall we philosophize, or just eat the cake?

Sizzle of meaning in every bite,
Sauce on the side, it feels so right.
In every crunch, a truth to unfold,
Or is it just fries, a story retold?

Questions Seasoned with Salt

Why are we here? A question with fries,
Underneath the seasoning, the truth lies.
Salt sprinkled questions dance on the plate,
As we munch on the unlikely fate.

Burgers and pondering, life's messy feast,
In the greased-up chaos, we laugh, not feast.
And as the last fry hits the shallow grave,
We toast to the questions, a life we crave.

The Absurdity of Eating Alone

A burger on the plate, it stares back,
Why does it feel like a midnight snack?
Fork in hand, a friendless affair,
I chuckle at the thoughts I bear.

Pickles and cheese, my silent crew,
Inanimate pals, a strange viewing clue.
Conversations with fries, all in my head,
A feast of absurdity, I'm joyfully fed.

Shadows of a Snack

Chips under the light, they beckon my soul,
The crunch and the munch, they take their toll.
Reflections in ketchup, a red-colored fate,
The shadows of snacks make me contemplate.

Lurking in corners, my nachos conspire,
Whisper sweet nothings, set my heart afire.
I ponder my purpose with each cheesy bite,
Nibbles of wisdom in the dead of night.

Midnight Musings and Munchies

In the quiet of night, the fridge opens wide,
 A smorgasbord view, my hungry pride.
Pretzels and popcorn, a philosophical feast,
 I question my being, yet snack like a beast.

Peanut butter dreams dance on bread,
I wonder if trees feel the weight of my spread?
Each bite's a dilemma, each crunch a thought,
The answers elusive, but oh, what I've sought!

A Dance with Delusion

Twisting my fries like they're dancing with grace,
In a world of confusion, we're keeping pace.
A milkshake serenade, swirling through air,
I dance with my doubts, without a care.

Onion rings twirl, a partner for night,
The glimmering ketchup, a spotlight so bright.
With every dip, I'm lost in the song,
The rhythm of munching, where I feel I belong.

A Philosophical Platter

In the café of thought, we munch,
While pondering life's big crunch.
With every fry dipped in a shake,
We question choices that we make.

Ketchup dreams and mustard fears,
We laugh while sipping on our beers.
Thoughts fry up like golden chips,
As wit flows from our salted lips.

A burger's bite reveals it all,
As condiments begin to sprawl.
Between the bites, a truth we see,
Philosophy tastes best with brie.

So let's debate while we consume,
The meaning wrapped in foil and gloom.
Peering deep in every dish,
For life's odd quirks, we add a wish.

Gastronomy of the Mind

Nibbling thoughts on paper plates,
Wondering if fries have fates.
A side of laughter, deep-fried glee,
As we dip into absurdity.

With every burger, a new dilemma,
Is the bun the real enigma?
Saucy wisdom, chili flare,
Gastronomic dreams float in the air.

Gravy flows like our swirling thoughts,
With every bite, the world is fought.
Crunchy truths in crispy bites,
We ponder the universe by the lights.

Between the sips of fizzy drinks,
Come radical ideas, as the brain blinks.
Philosophers munch side by side,
Delighting in this tasty ride.

Surreal Crisps in a Real World

With surreal tastes on a real plate,
Each fry whispers, "Don't hesitate!"
Fries transform the mundane spry,
As burgers become our alibi.

Waffle cones hold the wisdom's scoop,
In ketchup pools, we dance and stoop.
Crispy hazards in this buffet,
We laugh at the absurdity of the fray.

Life's a fast-food drive-thru lane,
Where dreams blend with greasy gain.
So take a bite, poke a bit of fun,
In this odd banquet, we have won.

Beneath the haze of onion rings,
Lies a truth that twists and clings.
The chips are crunchy, stories swell,
In our playful snack time, all is well.

The Ephemeral Nature of Snack Time

Whispers of popcorn fill the air,
Fleeting moments fully bare.
A donut's hole, a cosmic void,
In every bite, joy's employed.

Quick fries dance on the plate,
Holding secrets we contemplate.
The nachos shout, "Life's a blast!"
Each crunchy chip, a shadow cast.

Our snack time fades like fleeting thought,
Each dipping sauce, a lesson taught.
The cheese flows like time, so slick,
In savory bites, we find the trick.

Between the laughter and the crumbs,
Life rushes by, and still it hums.
In every fry, a moment's grace,
As we savor the absurd pace.

Between the Bun and the Beyond

In shadows cast by sesame seeds,
We ponder life and ketchup needs.
The pickle speaks of worlds unknown,
While mustard flows, a thoughtful tone.

A bite reveals the secret fate,
What's on the side, delicious plate.
With mayonnaise, we ask the sky,
Is this the truth or just a lie?

As fries heap high in paper boats,
We float along in gravy moats.
In every crunch and salty cheer,
Does the universe hold us dear?

So here we munch and sip our drink,
Finding meaning with each wink.
Between the bun, we search and find,
Life's absurd yet oh so kind.

What Lies Beneath the Grease

Beneath the sizzle and the steam,
Fried potato whispers dreams.
Each crumb a clue to life's grand quest,
With every dip, we're truly blessed.

The fryer hums a tuneful jig,
As questions rise like cake so big.
Is purpose just a sauce to taste?
Or do we simply, gladly waste?

A burger's hope, a taco's fear,
The veggies watch, but shed no tear.
In grease we trust and crunchy bite,
Philosophy takes flight tonight!

So munch we must, with laughter loud,
In diners dreams, we're ever proud.
For in this feast, we float and twirl,
The meaning's there, in every whirl.

Impulses of the Hungry Mind

A rumble comes, a call to fries,
The clock strikes noon, oh how time flies!
Thoughts like onions, layered deep,
In crispy shells, our troubles creep.

The craving sparks a wild debate,
Is life a meal, or just the plate?
Drowning thoughts in creamy dip,
Philosophy's a tasty trip.

As burgers stack in towering grace,
We question if we've found our place.
Each bite a ponder, every sip,
Are we the sauce or just the whip?

With playful bites and laughter shared,
We find the joy, no longer scared.
In every morsel, truth combined,
The essence of the hungry mind.

Another Life, Another Fry

In golden dreams of snack attack,
What if we chose another snack?
A shake, a pie, a side of zest,
Each option feels like life's own test.

With every crunch, we taste regret,
But laughter comes, we're not done yet!
What if the fries dreamed of more?
In playful mirth, we must explore.

The burger winks, the coleslaw grins,
In this chaos, life begins.
For every dip and every chance,
We find our truth in crispy dance.

So take a bite, let's have some fun,
In this mad world, we've just begun.
Another life, so near, so sly,
Each moment fried, we'll cheer and fly.

Midnight Reflections at the Diner

The neon lights flicker, a dance of despair,
As we ponder if life's just a greasy affair.
A burger reflects on its meaty own fate,
While I sip my coffee—bitter, yet great.

Consider the ketchup, like dreams on a plate,
Splashing around, oh, the beauty of fate!
With each dip in the fries, laughter unfolds,
As we chew on our worries, hot and cold.

The clock ticks not, on the toast lightly grilled,
We toast to existence, and fries are fulfilled.
Oh, what's the purpose? Who really can tell?
Just pass me more mayo, and serve me this swell!

In booths filled with laughter, we feast hand in hand,
Contemplating life's order—do we even understand?
The jukebox is playing our existential theme,
While I ponder if ketchup is really a dream.

Relishing Life's Fleeting Bites

Chasing after moments like fries on the floor,
Each crunch tells a story; oh, what's in store?
With every last sip of this fizzy delight,
I muse on existence, with laughter in flight.

The waiter walks by with a grin and a wink,
Like a philosopher pondering—what do we think?
A side of confusion, with a sprinkle of glee,
How's it all matter when I'm munching on Z?

A milkshake obscures my thoughts pure and bright,
As life's rapid twists make the silly feel right.
I joke with my fries, they wink back in delight,
"Hey buddy, we're all just snacks in the night!"

So let's raise a toast to this delightful charade,
With burgers and banter, a feast is displayed.
For if life's a platter, let's savor each bite,
In this diner of dreams, we toast to the night!

The Depths of Diner Conversation

Two souls at a table with nothing profound,
Discussing the ketchup—sweet, tangy, renowned.
"Is your life a burger?" one asks with a grin,
"Or are we just fries that the universe spins?"

Crumbling the napkins, the thoughts start to flow,
Between bites of the special, what do we know?
The coffee spills secrets, the creamer's a tease,
Are we lost in reflections or just lost in our cheese?

The waitress rolls by, with a tray full of fate,
"Just remember, dear friends, it's never too late!"
She laughs at our musings, no rules in her game,
Just fries, and a milkshake, "Who's to blame?"

In the depths of this diner, absurd is the norm,
As we waffle with questions, the laughter keeps warm.
So what's in the end? Just a whimsical pie,
With sides of deep thoughts, that we all must try!

Fries of Fortune and Folly

In a world where potatoes hold secrets untold,
Fries of fortune and folly, crispy and bold.
Each bite is a gamble, a chance we all take,
Dipped deep in those sauces, oh what a mistake!

We laugh at the universe, so vast yet so small,
While juggling our burgers, we dare to stand tall.
"Are we meant to savor or merely survive?"
Sipping soda wisdom, we thrive and contrive.

A side of absurdity, sprinkled with fun,
In the booth of the thinking, where bright thoughts run.
With ketchup as muse and a diet of dreams,
We snack on existence, unravel our schemes.

So let's toast with our fries, in this diner divine,
For life is a platter—it's yours and it's mine.
As we ponder the meaning, let laughs take their flight,
With each crunchy morsel, we embrace the delight!

Existential Crunch

In this vast land of salt and grease,
We ponder life, yet munch with ease.
Burgers sigh, while fries debate,
Do we choose our fate on this plate?

The ketchup smiles, it feels so bright,
But what's the meaning of this bite?
Sizzling questions, crispy thoughts,
In this kitchen, truth is sought.

Our lives may fry, or sizzle slow,
Yet rhythms dance in grease's flow.
Chasing nachos, dodging despair,
In every crunch, we find our flare.

So raise your fry, and join the jest,
For life's a feast, a funny quest.
In every dip, a laugh combined,
A crispy truth we leave behind.

Reflections in a Greasy Film

The mirror shows a face so fried,
With mustard dreams that slip and slide.
Between the bites of saggy bread,
I ponder why I'm still not dead.

Beneath the surface, oil gleams,
Our thoughts get lost in ketchup dreams.
The burger smiles, but I can't tell,
Am I in love, or just in hell?

Every greasy layer tells a tale,
Fries whisper low, like a flying whale.
Do we embrace, or just let go?
In the fryer's whirl, the answers flow.

So flip that patty, let's have fun,
Philosophy served with extra bun.
Life's a joke, we laugh and we cry,
In this greasy film, we'll learn to fly.

A Side of Reflection

With every order, served with flair,
I wonder if my life's laid bare.
The pickle winks, the soda sings,
In this diner, joy surely clings.

Beneath the cheese, the wisdom hides,
What lives inside this crispy guise?
A tater tot, with dreams so bold,
A side of truth, in stories told.

I take a bite, and ponder loud,
Am I just part of this hungry crowd?
Yet in the grease, I start to see,
The humor wrapped in mystery.

So let's embrace the thrilling ride,
With every meal, and silly stride.
It's nourished laughter that we crave,
In each reflection, the brave will save.

The Fryer's Paradox

In the fryer's hum, we seek the wise,
Crispy truths hide in golden guise.
Do we fry to live, or live to fry?
Beneath this surface, we wave goodbye.

A tinge of salt, an ounce of fate,
Are we the meal, or just the plate?
With every serve, life's questions tease,
Do we find peace amidst the cheese?

The fryer bubbles, thoughts collide,
In patties round, we must confide.
Between the crunch and tender ends,
Existence whirls, and laughter bends.

So here we fry, with joy, no doubt,
Life's a banquet, let's sing it out.
In every bite, a paradox thrives,
In cooking's warmth, we find our lives.

Talking Taters and Truths

In the kitchen, they chatter, warm and golden,
Spud philosophy, lightly beholden.
"Why do we fry?" one potato muses,
As the others nod, avoiding excuses.

Ketchup joins in, a tangy debate,
"Life's too short to just contemplate!"
"Drown your worries in ranch or oil!"
They delight in their crispy, flavorful toil.

A wise old fry speaks, "Just take a bite,
All your troubles will vanish from sight."
The pan sizzles loud, a lively affair,
While the fate of the bowl hangs in the air.

Crispy thoughts, all fried up by the heat,
In this culinary chaos, we can't retreat.
So let's embrace fun in each tasty bite,
For in every crunch, truths come to light.

Echoes of a Flavorful Anxiety

In a diner booth, ketchup spills wide,
Fries whisper secrets, nowhere to hide.
"What's it all for?" one fry cries out,
As the salt shaker sneers, full of doubt.

Grease-soaked musings drift through the air,
"Life's a short order, but who really cares?"
Onions ring in with a crispy perdition,
As they ponder their deep-fried condition.

"Should we stay golden?" one fry laments,
"Or risk the fryer for some new events?"
Laughter erupts, sweet and absurd,
Among starchy philosophers, truth's still blurred.

When the plate is empty, the chatter subsides,
Yet echoes persist, where flavor resides.
So munch on those worries, with laughter and cheer,
In the greasy abyss, we conquer our fear.

Unpacking the Fry Box of Life

A box of fries, a wonderscape,
A salty journey, no need for a cape.
"What's our purpose?" one fry inquires,
Boiling in oil, stoking desires.

Sauces stand tall, ready to explain,
"Drench us or dip us, we'll soothe your pain!"
In this cardboard cosmos, we dig and dive,
Each bite a question, does it help us thrive?

"Who knew spuds could muse so deep?"
The fries laugh lightly, no time for sleep.
With every crunch, a giggly delight,
Chasing uncertainty into the night.

So let's unwrap truths like we unwrap fries,
With a crunch of humor, who needs the skies?
Together we snack, and in each shared fry,
We find nuggets of joy, as life rolls by.

The Snack that Spars with Certainty

A platter of fries, so bold and bright,
Questioning life with each crispy bite.
"What'd you come for?" the mayo demands,
As a fry declares, "Let's start new plans!"

In a world of condiments, we grab and toss,
Fry debates are sweet, but often gloss.
"Am I a snack or a meal on my own?"
The hash browns chuckle, feeling overblown.

"Life's full of grease, nearly divine!"
Laughter erupts—our souls intertwine.
So sprinkle some salt and bring on the fun,
For in this fry chat, we're all number one.

With peanut butter, aioli, or plain,
Each bite a gamble, driving us sane.
In the snack of existence, take a chance,
Let's grapple with nonsense, it's time to dance!

Searching for Harmony in a Paper Bag

In the depths of hunger, I seek a prize,
A crinkly bag beneath the worldly skies.
Potatoes fried golden, a glorious find,
Yet where's the deep meaning amidst all the rind?

I ponder my choices, the salt, the crunch,
Fried fortune waiting for me to munch.
Is this blissful bite life's true grand plan?
Or just crisp delights tossed in a frying pan?

As I chomp on my joy, it spills like a song,
But what if my fate feels a little wrong?
Is happiness hidden in grease and despair?
Or merely a dip in the depths of thin air?

The napkin's my guide, it captures my tears,
In ketchup I drown all my flaky fears.
Between bites of laughter and crunches of fate,
I find life's odd harmony, I can't hesitate!

The Dish of Despair

On a cloudy Thursday, I dream of a meal,
A burger that whispers, 'I'm part of your feel.'
But awaits an empty plate, a joke on my plate,
In this comedic tragedy, I ponder my fate.

Fries line up like soldiers, all crispy and neat,
Yet they're silent companions in this culinary feat.
With each bite of sorrow, a chuckle emerges,
A delicious blend of remorse and small surges.

The ketchup's a canvas where my dreams go to play,
With flavors of life that just slip away.
Is my snack a reflection of existential dread?
Or just afternoon munchies creeping under my bed?

The plate looks back, with a wink and a sigh,
"Dear friend, don't you worry, just savor, don't cry."
For dessert lies in laughter, not found in the dish,
Just fries filled with humor, fulfilling that wish.

Indulgence in the Abyss

Down in the alley where shadows confess,
The fryer hums gently, it knows my stress.
I scoop up the darkness, a bucket of fries,
As they tumble and twinkle, my hunger replies.

The mayo looks thoughtful, the chili just grins,
As I ponder my being and why I am thin.
With each crispy crunch, I dance with despair,
Yet I find joy in the flavors that dare.

Life's absurdity fried in hot oil and salt,
Among trays of delight, is there really a fault?
Each dip of my fry is a question I crave,
Am I sweet, am I salty, or just fiercely brave?

In this smoky abyss, I sit and I munch,
With laughter and fries, I indulge in my hunch.
For the deeper I dip, the lighter I feel,
In a world made of fries, my truth's on a reel.

The Frying Pan and the Infinite

In a world full of pans, my mind starts to swirl,
With visions of fries taking over the whirl.
I ponder the cosmos, the why, and the when,
While crispy delights call—who could leave them, then?

From the sizzle of fat to the cool touch of dreams,
Life's absurdities unfold in small steamy beams.
The fryer is glowing, inviting and bright,
A portal to ponder, in daylight's dim light.

Do I seek out the answers in cheese-drenched delight?
Am I merely a fry lost in this chaotic fight?
Yet laughter erupts from the grease on my hands,
As I cherish the moments that life truly spans.

Each batch pouring forth feels endless and bold,
In a dance of existence, mine's worth more than gold.
So I twirl with my fries, with a grin on my face,
For the frying pan holds true harmony's grace.

Free Will and Fast Food

In a world of choices, I stand and stare,
Burgers beckon, but I'm in despair.
To eat a salad or a double fry,
The clock is ticking, oh me, oh my!

Each bite a question, each dip a chance,
I ponder my fate in a greasy dance.
Do I choose wisely or just choose to munch?
Welcome to chaos, let's grab some lunch!

Napkin in hand, I'm ready to roam,
Conscious of calories, far from home.
But life's too short to count every bite,
So I'll take the fries with that burger delight.

As I clash with my conscience, who will I blame?
The pickles or mayo, the mustard or shame?
In the drive-thru line, where dreams come alive,
I wave my flag for philosophy to thrive.

The Weight of Crispy Awareness

Crispy delight on my plate, oh what a tease,
Amidst this bounty, I ponder with ease.
Is life a buffet or the fast food craze?
Deep-fried questions swirl in a daze.

Fries stacked high, a monument bold,
To the meaning of being, or so I'm told.
Are they crunchy whispers or echoes of fate?
A side of philosophy; let's not be late!

With ranch or ketchup, I take my stand,
To dive into sauce, it's all so grand.
Awareness is heavy, yet tastes like bliss,
I savor each fry, it's a moment I miss.

So I'll crunch the absurdity, nibble the wise,
While grappling thoughts of the ultimate fries.
Life's slippery slope is just like this meal,
Full of questions and crunch, taste and feel.

Whispers from the Ketchup Bottle

In the fridge lies a bottle of secrets untold,
Whispers of tomato, both spicy and bold.
As I squeeze out my thoughts, they dribble and flow,
What's the meaning of burgers? It's tough to know!

The ketchup confesses of love and despair,
Of fries that are lonely, and chips that don't care.
What's the point of it all, when dipped in red bliss?
To ponder existence or simply to miss?

It's more than a condiment, it's deep, it's profound,
Like friendships that fizzle when bacon is downed.
So I drizzle on wisdom as I take a test bite,
In the diner of life, I'm ready to fight.

Ketchup in hand, I philosophize deep,
The journey is messy, the flavors we keep.
Each squeeze of the bottle, a choice that I make,
To savor the moment, for laughing's our fate.

Absurdity and Condiments

In the land of odd sauces, I play little games,
Mixing the flavors, redefining names.
Mustard of madness, relish of thought,
A side of absurdity, just what I sought.

Chili on fries, with a dash of the strange,
Life's twisted humor, it's all in the change.
Between bites and laughter, I question it all,
Is the universe random, or am I just small?

With every new combo that tests my delight,
I ponder the meaning of wrong and of right.
A dollop of chaos, a sprinkle of fun,
In this quirky diner, we're all on the run.

So raise up your ketchup, your mayo, your cheese!
Let's toast to the nonsense, 'cause it's sure to please.
In a world full of flavors both salty and sweet,
Absurdity reigns, life's not a defeat!

Fries and the Fragility of Meaning

In a world of golden streaks,
We ponder, are we mere techniques?
As ketchup flows and laughter extends,
We dip our thoughts, where joy transcends.

With every crunch, life's questions rise,
Salted truths beneath the skies.
Beneath the surface, deep we fry,
Yet in each bite, we just comply.

Oh, the potatofied conundrum!
To snack or not—what's come undone?
In greasy pools, our laughs are found,
In crispy edges, meaning is drowned.

So grab a tub, embrace the jest,
In frying oil, we'll take our rest.
For in the folds of every fry,
We find both reason, and a pie.

Crispy Cravings and Cosmic Queries

What if the stars were potato skins?
We'd ponder life with cheeky grins.
In every crunch, the universe calls,
As crispy cravings dance in the halls.

We're lost in thoughts of fryer fate,
Are we just snacks upon a plate?
With every munch, we find new dread,
While chasing dreams of melted spread.

Lunar fries, stellar dips,
Every bite—a cosmic quip.
And as we savor each delight,
We giggle at the endless night.

Let's toss our doubts in frying oil,
And let our worries start to spoil.
With every taste, the humor's real,
In crispy layers, we begin to feel.

In Search of the Perfect Dipping Sauce

The quest for sauce, oh what a plight,
Is ranch a dream or just a bite?
In hidden realms of flavor's best,
We seek the truth, a crispy quest.

With mayo dreams and salsa schemes,
We probe the depths of saucy beams.
Sweet and tangy, or spicy flair,
In every dip, we show we care.

The existential fry reveals,
The sauce of life, how it appeals.
In vats of flavor, laughs emerge,
As questions swirl and thoughts converge.

So grab a fry and test the blend,
Will it fulfill, or just offend?
In every dip, we find a trace,
Of crispy thoughts in a saucy space.

Fleeting Moments and Fried Potatoes

Life's but a fry, crisp on the outside,
Moments so fleeting, they tend to hide.
As potatoes sizzle in bubbling glee,
We laugh at the absurdity of 'me'.

Catch the glaze as they slide and pop,
Epicurean dreams that never stop.
With every bite, the timer ticks,
Fried in oil, in laughter, we mix.

So raise your fry, toast to the odd,
In this circus where thoughts can applaud.
The golden treats remind us to grin,
In fleeting moments, life's best is within.

Potato platters in timeless dance,
In every crunch, we find a chance.
With grease on our hands, we savor the spree,
For in this fun, we are truly free.

Composed in a Constellation of Fry

In a galaxy of grease so divine,
Potatoes float, all forms intertwine.
Cosmic crunch calls from afar,
A bag of joy, a shining star.

Lost in thoughts of golden bliss,
A crispy center, a savory kiss.
Minds may wander, but hearts are sound,
In ketchup rivers, freedom found.

Bites of Ambiguity

Fries or philosophy? What's the key?
Dipping in sauces, pondering free.
Life's such a riddle, a simple crunch,
Finding your truth with each tasty munch.

Are we meant to share, or just eat alone?
Fries unite us, even through the unknown.
Each bite a question, crispy and light,
In mystery's embrace, we take our flight.

A Taste of Transcendence

In the fryer's heat, spirits ignite,
Potato dreams take off in the night.
Salty wisdom spills on the plate,
Crunchy insights, we contemplate.

Ever searching for that perfect dip,
Life's a platter, take a nibble, not a sip.
Cheese dreams melt in the cosmos' sway,
Who knew fries could brighten the day?

Musing with a Side of Sauce

Philosophers chat over a hot tray,
What's the essence of fries in play?
Mayonnaise or mustard, which do I choose?
In sauce we trust, with nothing to lose.

Between each crunch, the laughter flows,
What is the meaning? Nobody knows.
In a world of flavor, we dance and sway,
Life's agony melts in a side of aioli today.

Fryer of the Mind

Deep in the fryer, thoughts swirl and dance,
Sizzle and pop, they take a chance.
Is life a potato, or just a blob?
A crispy question, served with a sob.

Flipping through memories like greasy fries,
Wondering if truth wears a cunning disguise.
With each golden bite, I ponder and chew,
Is the ketchup the answer, or just good for stew?

The Search for Satisfying Absurdity

In a world of burgers, we quest for the fries,
Searching for meaning in grease-coated pies.
Like a clown in a circus, juggling our plight,
Finding the punchline in the dead of the night.

Each bite's a riddle, absurd yet so sweet,
With crispy delights, isn't life quite the treat?
Drowning in mayo, we laugh as we fry,
In the kitchen of chaos, we all learn to fly.

Beneath the Surface of Simplicity

Under the surface where secrets reside,
Lies a world of potatoes, their dreams open wide.
Mashed or fried, they ponder their fate,
Simply complex, they navigate fate.

There's wisdom in quick orders if you look,
Beneath the fast food, mysteries cook.
A side of coleslaw, perhaps a crisp turn,
In the funhouse mirror, we all take a burn.

Crispy Thoughts on a Soft Bun

Thoughts like toppings, piled high on the bread,
Each one a giggle, or something unsaid.
With lettuce of doubt, and tomatoes of cheer,
We munch on our musings, with fries always near.

In the blend of flavors, the absurd is served,
A feast of confusion, yet we're so unnerved.
Between bites of laughter and snorts of delight,
Our crispy conclusions take flight in the night.

Juxtaposition of Crunch and Thought

In the diner of dreams, we munch our way,
Philosophers feast, as the fryers sway.
A potato's plight, we ponder deep,
While ketchup laughs, and pickles peep.

Between bites of wisdom, our minds collide,
With crispy truths, we cannot hide.
Salted reflections on plates of gold,
Questions linger, as stories unfold.

A burger grips the weight of fate,
What's the meaning of this cheeseburger plate?
Fries in hand, we toast to the night,
Life's absurdities feel strangely right.

Burgers ponder, and shakes may sigh,
With every crunch, we reach for the sky.
In laughter and grease, we find our way,
Philosophy served, one fry at a play.

The Greasy Path to Understanding

Wandering through a world of fries,
We seek the truth behind the lies.
What do the onions really see?
As they join the dance, so joyfully.

A burger smirks, in all its grace,
A bun's soft pillow, a warm embrace.
With every dip into that sauce,
We weigh our thoughts and count the cost.

Lost in the haze of deep-fried fate,
Each bite a question, each crunch a fate.
Life's a drive-thru winding, a twist,
Where answers blur, and nothing's missed.

So let loose your thoughts, and eat with glee,
As fries reveal what's hard to see.
Munching away, let laughter ring,
On this greasy path, we find our zing.

Fragments of a Frying Pan Philosophy

In the sizzle of oil, wisdom drips,
With every fry, our thinking flips.
A platter of chaos, all stacked high,
Crunching through meaning, we can't deny.

A philosopher's hat made of cheese,
Worn with a smile, aiming to please.
In the midst of crumbs, we giggle and muse,
While the mayo ponders, which way to choose?

Like cold fries forgotten on a plate,
Questions linger, they can't wait.
With a side of laughter, truths do sprout,
In this greasy pan, we laugh about.

So dip into thoughts as we feast on fries,
Where laughter's the answer, no need for lies.
Fragments of wisdom, drizzled in fun,
Philosophy's cool, with ketchup, we run.

In the Shadows of the Snack Bar

In the shadows of snacks, we hold debates,
Tater tots whisper, and cheese curds wait.
Philosophy lingers in the air,
While burgers ponder their crispy hair.

A salt shaker laughs, wise and old,
It sprinkles truths that are bold and gold.
Fries huddle close, in a secret place,
Sharing laughs about the human race.

With dips and sauces, we swirl around,
In this snack bar world, confusion's found.
Chillin' with chips, we ponder our fate,
What's real and what's just good on a plate?

So raise your fries in a toast to the odd,
In every bite, we find something flawed.
Laughter echoes, bright and free,
In the shadows of snacks, the truth's a spree.

www.ingramcontent.com/pod-product-compliance
Lightning Source LLC
Chambersburg PA
CBHW051636160426
43209CB00004B/668